THOMAS WEST

Ice Hockey for Newbies

Understanding the game for the new fan

First edition

This book was professionally typeset on Reedsy.
Find out more at reedsy.com

Contents

1

Introduction

Ice hockey is a fast-paced, physical sport that is popular around the world. Played on a sheet of ice with a puck and sticks, the objective of the game is to score more goals than the opposing team. Whether you're a newcomer to the sport or even a seasoned fan looking to brush up on the basics, this book will provide a comprehensive guide to the history of ice hockey, rules, and strategies of the game.

Chapter 1: History of the game

The history of ice hockey can be traced back to the 19th century, when it was first played in Canada. The exact origins of the game are unclear, but it is believed to have been inspired by similar stick-and-ball games played in Europe.

The first organized indoor game of ice hockey was played in Montreal in 1875, and the first set of rules for the game were developed shortly thereafter. The game quickly gained popularity in Canada, and by the turn of the 20th century, it had become the country's national sport.

In 1892, the first Stanley Cup championship was held, with the Montreal Canadiens emerging as the champions. The Stanley Cup is still awarded to the winners of the NHL playoffs each year, and it is considered one of the most prestigious trophies in sports.

Ice hockey continued to grow in popularity throughout the early 20th century, with the formation of several professional leagues in North America. The National Hockey League (NHL) was founded in 1917, and it remains the premier professional hockey league in the world today.

During the mid-20th century, ice hockey also began to gain popularity in Europe, with several countries forming their own professional leagues. The Soviet Union emerged as a dominant force in international ice hockey, winning numerous Olympic and World Championship titles during the 1950s and 1960s.

In the 1970s and 1980s, the NHL began to expand beyond its traditional base in Canada and the northeastern United States, with teams being added in cities such as Los Angeles and San Jose. This expansion helped to popularize the sport in new markets, and it helped to increase the NHL's overall revenue and exposure.

The 1990s and 2000s saw further expansion of the sport, with the NHL adding teams in cities such as Dallas, Phoenix, Nashville, and Atlanta. The sport also continued to grow in popularity internationally, with the formation of the Kontinental Hockey League (KHL) in Russia and the expansion of the Swedish Hockey League (SHL) and Finnish Liiga.

Today, ice hockey is played and enjoyed by millions of people all over the world. It is one of the most exciting and fast-paced sports in existence, with a rich history and tradition that continues to evolve and grow with each passing year. Whether you are a lifelong fan or a newcomer to the game, there is always something new to discover and appreciate about the sport of ice hockey.

Chapter 2: The Basics

I ce hockey is a fast-paced and physical sport that is played on an ice rink between two teams of six players each. The objective of the game is to score more goals than the opposing team by shooting a puck into their net while preventing the other team from doing the same.

The game is played in three periods, each lasting 20 minutes of actual playing time, with a 15-minute intermission between the second and third periods. If the game is tied at the end of regulation, it may go into overtime or a shootout to determine a winner.

The rink is divided into three zones: the offensive zone, the defensive zone, and the neutral zone. Each team has three forwards, two defensemen, and a goaltender. The forwards are responsible for generating offense and scoring goals, while the defensemen are responsible for protecting their own net and preventing the other team from scoring.

The game begins with a faceoff, where the puck is dropped between two opposing players in the center of the rink. From there, each team tries to gain possession of the puck and move it up the ice towards the opposing team's net. Players can use their sticks to pass the puck to each other, or they can carry it themselves by skating.

A player cannot touch the puck with their hands or feet, except for the goaltender who is allowed to use their hands to catch and handle the puck within the designated crease in front of their net. Players can also use their bodies to check or hit opposing players in an attempt to separate them from the puck.

Scoring a goal requires shooting the puck into the opposing team's net. If the puck completely crosses the goal line and enters the net, a goal is scored. If the goaltender stops the puck before it crosses the line or the puck hits the post or crossbar and does not cross the line, play continues.

Penalties are called by the officials for infractions such as tripping, slashing, or checking from behind. When a player is called for a penalty, they must serve time in the penalty box, and their team must play with one less player on the ice for the duration of the penalty.

The game of ice hockey is not just about individual skill, but also about teamwork, strategy, and physical toughness. Each player must work together with their teammates to outmaneuver and outscore the other team, while also defending their own net and preventing the other team from scoring.

In addition to the basic rules of the game, there are also several advanced techniques and strategies that players can employ to gain an advantage over their opponents. These include offensive plays such as the forecheck, which involves aggressively pursuing the puck in the offensive zone to create scoring opportunities, and defensive plays such as the trap, which involves clogging up the neutral zone to prevent the other team from entering the offensive zone.

Overall, ice hockey is a thrilling and exciting sport that requires skill, strategy, and physicality. Whether you are a casual fan or a die-hard supporter of a particular team, there is always something new and exciting to discover in the world of ice hockey.

4

Chapter 3: Scoring

S coring in ice hockey is the ultimate objective of the game. The team that scores the most goals by shooting the puck into the opposing team's net wins the game. Scoring a goal requires precision, skill, and teamwork.

A goal is scored when the puck completely crosses the goal line and enters the net. The goal line is the red line that extends across the width of the rink at both ends. The net is the structure that is located at each end of the rink and consists of a metal frame with a mesh netting that is designed to catch the puck.

To score a goal, a player must shoot the puck past the opposing team's goaltender and into their net. This can be done in a variety of ways, including shooting the puck with a wrist shot, slap shot, or backhand shot. A wrist shot involves quickly snapping the puck off the stick with the wrist, while a slap shot involves winding up and taking a powerful swing at the puck. A backhand shot is similar to a wrist shot but is taken with the backhand side of the stick.

Scoring a goal requires not only individual skill but also teamwork and strategy. Players must work together to set up scoring opportunities by passing the puck to each other and creating space on the ice. This often involves using quick and precise passes to catch the opposing team off guard and create openings in their defense.

The position of the player on the ice can also affect their ability to score a goal. Forwards are typically responsible for generating offense and are often the players who score the majority of the team's goals. They are positioned in the offensive zone and are often close to the opposing team's net, ready to take a shot when the opportunity arises. Defensemen, on the other hand, are responsible for protecting their own net and preventing the other team from scoring. They are positioned in the defensive zone and are often tasked with clearing the puck out of their own end and preventing the opposing team from setting up scoring opportunities.

Scoring a goal can also depend on the quality of the goaltender on both teams. Goaltenders are the last line of defense and are tasked with stopping the opposing team from scoring. They use a combination of quick reflexes, agility, and positioning to make saves and prevent the puck from entering their net.

Despite the importance of individual skill, scoring in ice hockey is often a team effort. A successful goal requires not only a well-placed shot but also effective passing, screening, and puck possession. Players must work together to create opportunities and capitalize on them when they arise.

In addition to scoring goals, players can also earn assists for their role in setting up a goal. An assist is awarded to the player who made the pass or contributed to the play that led to the goal. This recognizes the importance of teamwork in scoring and encourages players to work together to achieve success on the ice.

Overall, scoring in ice hockey is a complex and exciting aspect of the game. It requires skill, teamwork, and strategy, and can often be the difference between winning and losing. Whether you are a casual fan or a dedicated supporter of a particular team, watching a goal being scored is one of the most thrilling moments in the sport of ice hockey.

Chapter 4: Penalties

Penalties are an important part of ice hockey, as they help to enforce the rules of the game and maintain a level playing field. When a player breaks a rule, they may be assessed a penalty, which can result in their team being short handed and the opposing team having a power play.

There are two types of penalties in ice hockey: minor penalties and major penalties. Minor penalties are less severe and usually result in the offending player being sent to the penalty box for two minutes. Major penalties are more serious and can result in a player being ejected from the game or even suspended for multiple games. Some common reasons for penalties in ice hockey include tripping, hooking, slashing, and high-sticking. Tripping occurs when a player uses their stick or body to cause an opposing player to fall. Hooking occurs when a player uses their stick to impede the progress of an opposing player. Slashing occurs when a player strikes an opposing player with their stick. High-sticking occurs when a player hits an opposing player with their stick above the shoulders.

When a penalty is assessed, the offending player must serve their time in the penalty box, which is located next to the team benches. While the player is in the penalty box, their team is shorthanded, meaning they have one less player on the ice. This can make it more difficult for the shorthanded team to defend against the opposing team's offense and can lead to goals being scored against them. When a team is on a power play, they have an advantage because they have one more player on the ice than their opponents. This can make it easier for them to generate offense and score goals. Power plays usually last for two minutes, which is the amount of time a minor penalty is assessed for. If a team scores a goal while on a power play, the penalty is over and the offending player is allowed to return to the ice. However, if a major penalty is assessed, the player must serve the entire five-minute penalty, even if the opposing team scores a goal during that time.

In addition to minor and major penalties, there are also game misconduct penalties, which result in a player being ejected from the game. Game misconduct penalties are assessed for more serious offenses, such as fighting or intent to injure.

Overall, penalties play an important role in ice hockey by enforcing the rules of the game and maintaining a level playing field. While penalties can be frustrating for players and fans alike, they are necessary to ensure fair and safe competition. As a new fan of ice hockey, it's important to understand the various types of penalties and how they can impact the game.

Chapter 5: Faceoffs

F aceoffs are a crucial part of ice hockey and are used to restart play after a stoppage in the game. They are used to determine possession of the puck and are taken at the center of the rink, where the center red line intersects with the faceoff circles.

During a faceoff, two players from opposing teams' line up facing each other with their sticks on the ice. The linesman drops the puck between them, and the two players attempt to win possession of the puck by using their stick to try to control it and move it towards their team's players.

There are different types of faceoffs in ice hockey, and the location of the faceoff can depend on the reason for the stoppage in play. For example, if the puck goes out of bounds, the faceoff will occur in the nearest faceoff circle. If a penalty is assessed, the faceoff will occur in the defensive zone of the penalized team.

The most common type of faceoff is the center faceoff, which occurs at the start of each period and after a goal is scored. The center faceoff is taken by the two centers on each team, and winning the faceoff is crucial because it gives the team an opportunity to start the game or period with possession of the puck.

Another type of faceoff is the neutral zone faceoff, which occurs when there is a stoppage in play in the neutral zone, between the blue lines on the rink. The neutral zone faceoff is taken by one player from each team, and winning the faceoff can give the winning team a chance to gain control of the puck and create a scoring opportunity.

The defensive zone faceoff is taken in the defensive zone of the team that committed the infraction that led to the stoppage of play. The defensive zone faceoff is important because the defending team is often at a disadvantage, and winning the faceoff can help to prevent the opposing team from scoring a goal.

The offensive zone faceoff is taken in the offensive zone of the team that did not commit the infraction that led to the stoppage of play. The offensive zone faceoff is crucial because it gives the offensive team an opportunity to create scoring chances and potentially score a goal.

In addition to the different types of faceoffs, there are also strategies that teams can use to win faceoffs. For example, a team may use a different player to take the faceoff depending on the situation or may use specific tactics to try to win the faceoff, such as a "tie-up" or a "clean win". A tie-up is when a player tries to prevent the opposing player from gaining control of the puck by tying up their stick or body. A clean win is when a player wins the faceoff cleanly and is able to gain immediate control of the puck.

In conclusion, faceoffs are an important part of ice hockey and are used to restart play after a stoppage. Winning a faceoff can give a team possession of the puck and an opportunity to create scoring chances. Understanding the different types of faceoffs and strategies that teams use can help new fans appreciate this crucial aspect of the game.

Chapter 6: Icing the Puck

I cing the puck is a rule in ice hockey that occurs when a player shoots the puck from behind the center red line across the opposing team's goal line without it being touched by anyone. It is a violation that results in a stoppage in play and a faceoff in the defensive zone of the team that committed the infraction.

The purpose of the icing rule is to prevent teams from simply shooting the puck down the ice in an effort to kill time or gain an advantage without having to compete for the puck. It also encourages players to play the puck and create offensive opportunities, rather than just clearing the puck to the other end of the rink. When icing occurs, the linesman will blow the whistle to stop play, and a faceoff will take place in the defensive zone of the team that committed the infraction. This gives the opposing team an opportunity to try to score a goal or create a scoring opportunity, and it can put the team that committed the infraction at a disadvantage, as they cannot make any changes to their players on the ice until after the faceoff.

There are some exceptions to the icing rule. One exception is when a team is short-handed, or playing with a penalty, and they shoot the puck down the ice. In this case, the opposing team must touch the puck before the whistle will blow, allowing the short-handed team to potentially clear the puck and kill time. Another exception is when the goaltender of the team that committed the infraction is the first to reach the puck behind the goal line. In this case, the icing is waived off, and play continues, as the goaltender has shown the ability to play the puck and potentially prevent a scoring opportunity.

Icing the puck can also have tactical implications for teams. For example, if a team is under pressure in their defensive zone and cannot break out of their own end, they may choose to intentionally ice the puck to relieve the pressure and get their players a breather. However, this strategy can also backfire, as it gives the opposing team an opportunity to set up their offense and potentially score a goal. Additionally, icing the puck too frequently can result in a tired defensive team, as they will be forced to take more faceoffs in their own zone and defend more frequently.

In conclusion, icing the puck is a rule in ice hockey that occurs when a player shoots the puck from behind the center red line across the opposing team's goal line without it being touched by anyone. It is a violation that results in a stoppage in play and a faceoff in the defensive zone of the team that committed the infraction. Understanding the rules and implications of icing can help new fans appreciate the strategic and tactical aspects of the game.

Chapter 7: Strategies of the game

There are many different strategies that teams can use in ice hockey to gain an advantage over their opponents. In this chapter, we'll explore various scoring strategies for a new fan of ice hockey.

Forechecking

Forechecking is a strategy used by a team to pressure the opposing team's defense and create turnovers. The forechecking player's objective is to disrupt the opposing team's ability to move the puck up the ice and force them to make mistakes. This can lead to scoring opportunities for the forechecking team.

Cycling

Cycling is a strategy used by a team to maintain possession of the puck in the offensive zone. The players pass the puck around the boards and move to different positions to create passing lanes. This can create scoring opportunities as the players move the puck around the zone, looking for an opening to shoot or pass to a teammate.

Power Play

A power play occurs when one team has a player or players in the penalty box, giving the other team an advantage. The team with the advantage has more players on the ice, creating more scoring opportunities. The power play team will often use a set play to move the puck around the zone, looking for an opening to shoot or pass to a teammate.

Breakaway

A breakaway occurs when a player from one team gets past all of the opposing team's players and has a clear path to the net. This is an excellent scoring opportunity as the player has a one-on-one opportunity with the opposing team's goalie.

Rebound

A rebound occurs when a player shoots the puck at the net, and the goalie makes a save, but the puck rebounds back out into the play. The attacking team can then quickly shoot the puck again, taking advantage of the goalie being out of position.

Tip-In

A tip-in occurs when a player redirects a shot from a teammate into the net. This strategy is often used when the attacking team has players positioned in front of the opposing team's net. The redirected shot can catch the goalie off guard, leading to a goal.

One-Timer

A one-timer is a shot taken immediately after receiving a pass. This strategy is often used on the power play, as the attacking team can move the puck quickly around the zone, creating passing lanes and one-timer opportunities.

Wrap-Around

A wrap-around occurs when a player skates behind the opposing team's net with the puck and then attempts to stuff the puck into the net on the other side. This can be an effective scoring strategy as it catches the goalie off guard.

Deflection

A deflection occurs when a player redirects a shot from a teammate into the net with their stick or body. This strategy is often used when the attacking team has players positioned in front of the opposing team's net.

Slap Shot

A slap shot is a hard shot taken with a full wind-up and a sweeping motion of the stick. This strategy is often used from the point on the power play, as the attacking team can get a hard shot on net from a distance, creating rebound opportunities.

In conclusion, ice hockey is a sport that offers many different scoring strategies, each with its advantages and disadvantages. As a new fan, it's essential to understand these strategies to fully appreciate the game and the players' skills. With time and experience, you'll learn to recognize these strategies and appreciate the exciting moments that make ice hockey such a fantastic sport.

Chapter 8: Stanley Cup Playoffs

The NHL Stanley Cup playoffs are the pinnacle of professional ice hockey. The playoffs consist of four rounds of best-of-seven series, with the winner of each series advancing to the next round. The playoffs culminate in the Stanley Cup Final, where the two remaining teams face off to determine the NHL champion.

The playoffs are an exciting and intense time for both players and fans alike. The atmosphere in the arenas is electric, with fans cheering on their favorite teams and players. The pressure is high, and every game matters as teams battle it out for a chance to lift the Stanley Cup.

The first round of the playoffs, also known as the Conference Quarter-finals, features the top three teams from each division, along with two wild-card teams from each conference. The wild-card teams are the two teams with the most points in the conference who did not finish in the top three in their respective division. The Conference Quarterfinals are a best-of-seven series, with the higher-seeded team hosting the first two games, and the lower-seeded team hosting the next two games. If necessary, the final three games are played in a 2-2-1 format, with the higher-seeded team hosting the fifth and seventh games.

The second round of the playoffs, also known as the Conference Semifinals, features the winners of the Conference Quarterfinals. The format is the same as the first round, with the higher-seeded team hosting the first two games, and the lower-seeded team hosting the next two games. If necessary, the final three games are played in a 2-2-1 format, with the higher-seeded team hosting the fifth and seventh games.

The third round of the playoffs, also known as the Conference Finals, features the winners of the Conference Semifinals. The format is the same as the first two rounds, with the higher-seeded team hosting the first two games, and the lower-seeded team hosting the next two games. If necessary, the final three games are played in a 2-2-1 format, with the higher-seeded team hosting the fifth and seventh games.

The final round of the playoffs, known as the Stanley Cup Final, features the winners of the Conference Finals. The Stanley Cup Final is also a best-of-seven series, with the team with the better regular season record hosting the first two games, and the other team hosting the next two games. If necessary, the final three games are played in a 2-2-1 format, with the team with the better regular season record hosting the fifth and seventh games.

One of the unique aspects of the NHL Stanley Cup playoffs is the intensity of the games. With every game being a do-or-die situation, the pressure is high, and players must perform at their best. Teams must make strategic decisions and adjust their game plans to counter their opponents, making each game an exciting and unpredictable affair.

Another aspect of the playoffs that makes them so thrilling is the physicality of the game. Players are willing to sacrifice their bodies to make plays and win games, leading to some of the most intense and hard-hitting games of the season. The NHL Stanley Cup playoffs also provide fans with the opportunity to witness some of the greatest moments in hockey history. From iconic goals to incredible saves, the playoffs have produced some of the most memorable moments in the sport's history.

In conclusion, the NHL Stanley Cup playoffs are an exciting and intense time for both players and fans. With four rounds of best-of-seven series, the playoffs culminate in the Stanley Cup Final, where the two remaining teams battle it out for a chance to lift the Stanley Cup. The playoffs are a unique and thrilling experience, with the pressure and physicality of the games making each one a do-or-die situation.

10

Conclusion

I ce hockey is a thrilling and fast-paced sport that offers fans a unique experience. From the physicality of the game to the scoring strategies used by the teams, ice hockey is an exciting sport that captivates fans of all ages. For new fans, ice hockey provides an opportunity to experience a sport that is both challenging and entertaining.

One of the main reasons why ice hockey is such a wonderful sport for new fans is the energy and excitement that surrounds each game. The atmosphere in an ice hockey arena is electric, with fans cheering on their favorite teams and players. The sound of skates cutting through the ice and the crash of bodies against the boards adds to the excitement of the game.

Another reason why ice hockey is a fantastic sport for new fans is the physicality of the game. The sport is known for its hard hits, fights, and aggressive play. While some fans may find this aspect of the game off-putting, many others enjoy the adrenaline rush that comes with watching their favorite players lay a big hit on an opponent.

In addition to the physicality of the game, ice hockey also offers fans a variety of scoring strategies. From the forecheck to the one-timer, there are many different ways that teams can score goals in ice hockey. For new fans, learning about these different strategies and understanding how they are used can be an exciting and educational experience.

Ice hockey is also a sport that requires a great deal of skill and athleticism. From the speed and agility required to skate on the ice to the precision needed to shoot and pass the puck, ice hockey players are some of the most talented athletes in the world. For new fans, watching these athletes perform at the highest level can be both inspiring and awe-inspiring.

Finally, ice hockey is a sport that is steeped in tradition and history. From the Stanley Cup to the Original Six teams, there are many iconic aspects of the sport that fans have come to love and appreciate. For new fans, learning about the history of the sport and its iconic moments can add to their enjoyment and appreciation of the game.

Ice hockey is a fantastic sport for new fans to enjoy. From the energy and excitement of the game to the physicality and athleticism of the players, ice hockey offers a unique and thrilling experience. For those who are new to the sport, taking the time to learn about the different scoring strategies, the history of the game, and the players and teams involved can add to their enjoyment and appreciation of this wonderful sport. Whether you are a die-hard fan or just starting out, ice hockey is a sport that is sure to captivate and entertain.

If you found this book helpful, I'd be very appreciative if you left a favorable review for the book on Amazon!

Printed in Great Britain
by Amazon

38558290R00020